Animal Lives

TORTOISES AND TURTLES

Sally Morgan

Teacher Created Resources

Copyright © QEB Publishing, Inc. 2006

First published in the United States by
QEB Publishing, Inc.
23062 La Cadena Drive
Laguna Hills, CA 92653

This edition published by
Teacher Created Resources, Inc.
6421 Industry Way
Westminster, CA 92683

www.teachercreated.com

Library of Congress Control Number:
2005911037

ISBN 978-1-4206-8110-9

Written by Sally Morgan
Designed by Jonathan Vipond
Editor Hannah Ray
Picture Researcher Joanne Forrest Smith

Publisher Steve Evans
Art Director Zeta Davies
Editorial Director Jean Coppendale

Printed and bound in China

Picture Credits

Key: t=top, b=bottom, l=left, r=right,
FC = front cover

Ardea 16 /Ken Lucas 30bl; **Corbis** Anthony
Bannister/Gallo Images 10 /Wolfgang
Kaehler 5tr /David A Northcott 6 /Linda
Richardson 11 /Jeffrey L Rotman 28–29 /
C Rouvieres/Sygma 24–2 /Kevin Schafer 30tr
& tl /Kennan Ward 12; **Ecoscene** Jeff Collett
25tl /John Pitcher 23tr; **FLPA** Jim
Brandenburg/Minden Pictures 22–23 /
R Dirscher 19 /Patricio Robles Gil/Sierra
Madre/Minden Pictures 26 /Frans Lanting/
Minden Pictures 27 /Claus Meyer/Minden
Pictures 29tr /Chris Newbert/Minden Pictures
18 /Fritz Polking /Malcolm Schuyl 14;
Gettyimages Georgette Douwma FC; **NHPA**
/James Carmichael 1 /Nigel Dennis 8–9 /Ken
Griffiths 15tr /Hellio & Van Ingen 16–17 /Bill
Love 4–5 /Haroldo Palo Jr 20 /Linda Pitkin 15;
Still Pictures Fred Bruemmer 21 /C Allan
Morgan 13.

Words in **bold** are
explained in the
Glossary on page 31.

Contents

Tortoises and turtles

Tortoises and turtles are **ancient** animals that first appeared on Earth more than 200 million years ago, when the dinosaurs were alive. Their appearance has changed very little in all this time. They are easy to recognize because they have a heavy shell covering their back.

This Cagle's map turtle has a flatter shell than a tortoise.

This giant tortoise has a heavy, domed shell and thick legs.

Reptiles

Turtles and tortoises are related to lizards, snakes, and crocodiles. They belong to a group of animals called **reptiles**, which have **scaly** skin and lay leathery eggs.

Tortoises are land animals, but turtles spend most of their life either in or by water. Freshwater turtles are found in rivers, lakes, and swamps, while sea turtles are found in the oceans. Some freshwater turtles are called **terrapins**, which means "little turtle."

5

Types of tortoise and turtle

Some tortoises and turtles, such as this snapping turtle, have extra armor on their shells.

There are about 290 **species**, or types, of tortoise and turtle, and all of them have a shell. There are a total of 60 bones in the shell, which is covered by large scales for extra protection. Turtles have a fairly flat shell, which is a better shape for swimming. Tortoises, however, have a domed shell that gives more protection from **predators**.

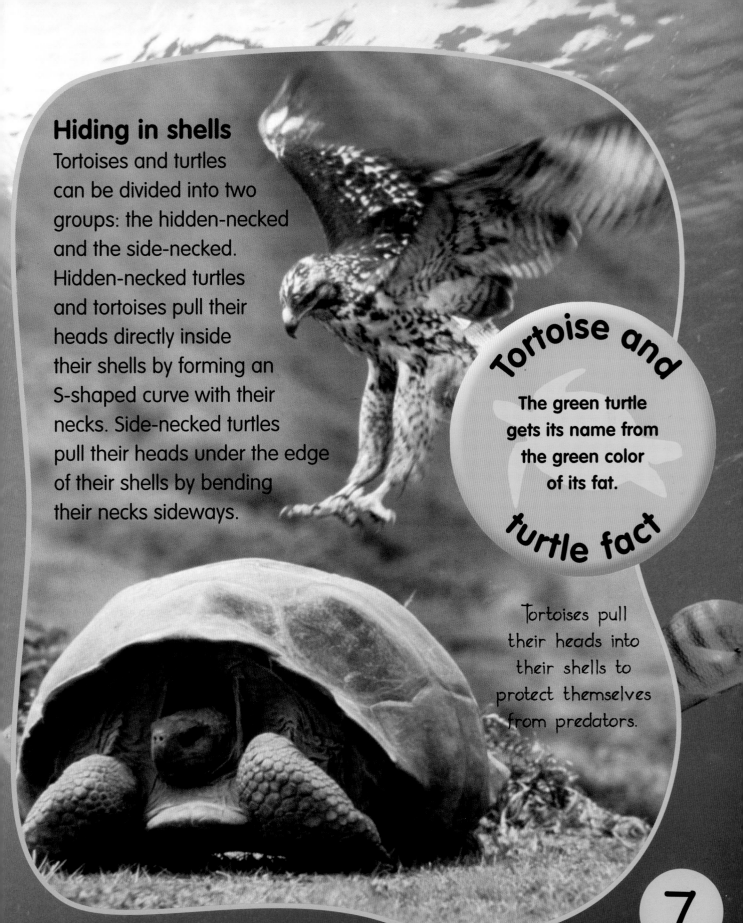

Hiding in shells

Tortoises and turtles can be divided into two groups: the hidden-necked and the side-necked. Hidden-necked turtles and tortoises pull their heads directly inside their shells by forming an S-shaped curve with their necks. Side-necked turtles pull their heads under the edge of their shells by bending their necks sideways.

Tortoise and turtle fact

The green turtle gets its name from the green color of its fat.

Tortoises pull their heads into their shells to protect themselves from predators.

Where can you find tortoises and turtles?

Leopard tortoises are found in Africa. They live in woodland areas and on the grasslands.

Tortoise and

Desert tortoises can survive for long periods without water. This is because they store water inside their bodies to use when they cannot find water.

turtle fact

Areas where turtles are found
Areas where tortoises are found

All over the world

Turtles and tortoises are found on every continent except Antarctica. Tortoises and freshwater turtles are found mainly in **tropical** and subtropical climates. The greatest variety of freshwater turtles can be found in the southern US and in India and Bangladesh, in Asia. Tortoises are also found in southern Europe.

Ocean living

Sea turtles are found mostly in tropical oceans, but some species swim far north, almost to the Arctic. They can be found in the deep ocean, too. Turtles do not have to come to the surface to breathe because they can take in oxygen from the water through their skin and throat. This means they can stay underwater for weeks at a time.

Beginning life

The female tortoise digs a hole in which she lays her eggs, and then she covers them.

Turtles and tortoises lay leathery eggs. The female tortoise or turtle lays between 1 and 240 eggs at a time, depending on her species. The time taken for the eggs to hatch also varies, from two months to more than a year.

10

Nesting on beaches

Female sea turtles return to the beach on which they were born to lay their eggs. At night, they haul themselves up onto the beach and dig a deep hole in the sand in which to lay their eggs. The eggs hatch a few months later, and the **hatchlings** dig their way to the surface. Most hatchlings emerge at night, when they are less likely to be seen by predators, and make a quick dash to the sea. Some sea turtles lay several **clutches** of eggs each year.

These hatchlings have made it to the safety of the water.

Growing up

Hatchlings look like miniature adults. They range in size from just 1 in. (2.5 cm) to about 3 in. (8 cm) long. They are on their own from the moment they hatch, because their parents do not look after them. Many of the young tortoises and turtles die during their first few years. A lot are eaten by predators, and others die through a lack of food. Young tortoises living in dry habitats may also die during droughts.

It takes these desert tortoises five years to grow to a length of just 3 in. (8 cm.)

Growth

Young tortoises and turtles grow rapidly during the first few years of their lives, but then their growth slows down. The smaller species stop growing when their shell reaches about 5 in. (13 cm) long. The larger species continue to grow throughout their lives.

Long lives

Once they are adults, the number of tortoises and turtles that die is very small. In fact, they have some of the longest life spans of any animals. Tortoises and turtles in captivity live to be about 70 years of age. In the wild, they live for 30 to 40 years. Some, however, live considerably longer. Box turtles, for example, can live for 100 years.

Scientists can age some turtles from growth marks on their scales.

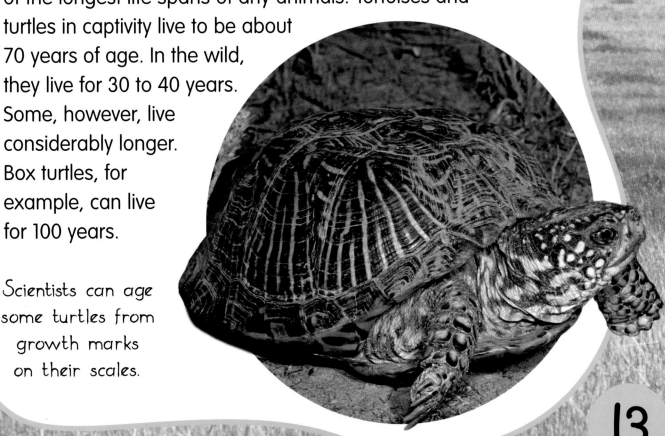

13

Getting around

Turtles and tortoises move around in different ways. Tortoises are well known for walking very slowly, but turtles can swim surprisingly quickly.

On land

Tortoises are adapted to moving on land. They have large feet with short toes. To walk, they raise their heavy bodies off the ground. Their walking speed is just 0.3 to 0.5 mph (0.5 to 0.8 km/h.)

Tortoises need sturdy legs to lift their heavy bodies off the ground.

In the water

Freshwater turtles have to be able to walk on land and swim in water. Many of these turtles live in shallow water and walk over the bottom of lakes or rivers. When they swim, they generally use all four legs as paddles.

Snake-necked turtles are found in Australia, where they live both on land and in water.

Sea turtles use their flippers to push themselves through the water.

At sea

Sea turtles spend their lives in the ocean and are powerful and graceful swimmers. Their shell has a flat shape that slips easily through the water. They have long toes that are joined together to form flipper-like paddles. They use their hind legs as a rudder for steering.

Tortoise and turtle senses

Tortoises and turtles have senses that enable them to find their way around and to find food. The senses of a turtle are slightly different from those of a tortoise, because turtles live in water.

Smell

Turtles have an excellent sense of smell, and this enables them to find food. They "smell" the water by opening their mouths slightly, drawing the water in through their noses, and pushing it out through their mouths.

Color vision helps this green turtle to find food on coral reefs.

Sight

Both tortoises and turtles have good eyesight and can see in color. Sight is important for finding food, and turtles and tortoises are particularly attracted to foods that are green, red, and yellow. Turtles' eyes have adapted so that they can see underwater, too.

Hearing

Tortoises can hear sounds, while turtles can feel **vibrations** in the water and this tells them where food, or a predator, might be.

Tortoise and turtle fact

When musk turtles are picked up they produce a very smelly substance from their skin to discourage predators.

Touch

Tortoises and turtles have a network of nerves that run over the surface of their shells. This means they can sense anything that touches them.

European pond turtles live in murky water, so they rely on their sense of smell and hearing to catch their **prey**.

17

Feeding

Adult green turtles are unusual as they feed only on plants such as algae and sea grass.

Tortoises and turtles do not have any teeth. Instead, they have a beak-like structure around their strong jaws. Tortoises eat mostly leaves, fruit, and slow-moving animals, such as snails and worms. Sea turtles eat a variety of animal foods including jellyfish, coral, sea urchins, crabs, and fish.

Tortoise and

The matamata, a type of freshwater turtle, lies in wait for a fish to come by. Then it opens its mouth wide and expands its throat, sucking the fish straight into its mouth!

turtle fact

Hunting

Tortoises and most freshwater turtles move too slowly to hunt prey. Some get around this problem by lying in wait for prey animals to pass by. One of the most aggressive turtles is the snapping turtle, which eats almost anything as long as it can catch and swallow it.

Sea turtles, such as this hawksbill, feed on jellyfish that float in the water.

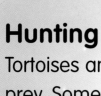

19

Predators

Predators, such as crabs, gather on the beach to catch and eat the turtle hatchlings.

Tortoises and turtles have many different predators. Their eggs are dug up and eaten by animals such as monitor lizards and raccoons, and hatchlings are eaten by birds and other animals.

As they get larger, turtles and tortoises are less likely to be attacked by other animals. Their shell patterns and colors give them **camouflage**, so it can be difficult to spot them. The domed shells of tortoises also makes it hard for a predator to grip the animal in its jaws.

Tortoise and turtle fact

The shell of the pancake tortoise from East Africa is very flat so it can squeeze into narrow crevices between rocks. Once it is wedged in place, it is impossible for a predator to pull it out.

Hunted

Humans are predators of turtles, too. In many parts of the world, people eat turtle meat and eggs. Some countries have banned this, but the hunting still goes on.

In places such as El Salvador, Guatemala, and Mexico, sea turtle eggs are dug up and sold as delicacies.

Ectothermic

Tortoises and turtles are **ectothermic**, or cold-blooded, animals. This means that their body temperature changes with the temperature of their surroundings. Ectothermic animals are only active when they are warm. In the morning, tortoises and freshwater turtles can be seen basking in the sun to warm up.

Tortoise and turtle fact

Horsfield's tortoise, which lives in Kazakhstan (central Asia), stays underground for nine months of the year. It emerges only when it rains and there is vegetation available for it to eat.

These painted turtles have climbed onto a log so they can sit in the sun and warm their bodies.

Hibernation

Tortoises and freshwater turtles that live in cooler temperate regions cannot survive outdoors in the cold winter months. The temperatures are too cold for them to be active, and there is no food. To survive, they go into a type of deep sleep called **hibernation**. Tortoises sleep in burrows in the ground. Freshwater turtles hibernate in mud at the bottom of ponds. They survive by absorbing oxygen from the water through their skin.

Eastern box turtles emerge from hibernation in April, when the weather is warmer.

Migrating turtles

Most freshwater turtles feed and nest in the same area. However, sea turtles make a long journey every year or so to return to the beaches where they were born and lay their eggs. This regular journey is called a **migration**.

Hundreds of female turtles have arrived at the same time to lay their eggs on this beach in Costa Rica.

Turtles, such as this hawksbill, navigate their way across huge oceans.

Finding their way

Scientists are unsure how the turtles manage to find their way across the oceans. It may involve smelling the water, or even using a sense that scientists do not yet know about.

Tortoise and

One of the largest gatherings of turtles occurs on a beach in India. More than 200,000 Olive Ridley turtles have been known to gather along a 3-mile (5 km) stretch of beach over a period of just two days.

turtle fact

Living alone

Most tortoises and turtles live a **solitary** life, only coming into contact with others when they feed in the same area or when they mate. Tortoises usually live in a particular area, called a territory. However, unlike many other animals that have territories, they do not defend their territory from other tortoises and so the territories of different tortoises may overlap.

Tortoise and turtle fact

Some turtles, such as roofed turtles and South American river turtles, clean each other. One turtle uses its jaws to pull algae off the other, and then they switch places.

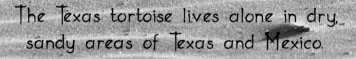

The Texas tortoise lives alone in dry, sandy areas of Texas and Mexico.

Reaching taller

There are a few species of tortoises that live in groups all the time, such as the giant tortoises of the Galapagos Islands. They have a hierarchy in which some individuals are more important than others. This is based on how high each tortoise can extend its head. A tortoise that can extend its head farther can reach more plants to eat, which means it grows larger.

Tortoises that can stretch their necks the farthest are more important within the group.

Tortoises and turtles under threat

Half of all the species of tortoises and turtles are at risk of becoming **extinct**. Tortoises have suffered from a loss of **habitat** and from being caught in the wild to be kept as pets. Sea turtles have had their breeding beaches disturbed by tourism and are also caught and eaten in many parts of Asia. Their eggs are also eaten. The shells of tortoises and turtles have been used to make jewelry, while the skin of the Olive Ridley turtle is used an expensive leather.

Some sea turtles get caught in fishing nets.

In some places, eggs are moved to conservation centers. When they have hatched, the hatchlings are released back into the water.

Conserving tortoises and turtles

Fortunately, people are trying to care for the remaining tortoises and turtles. Laws have been passed that make it illegal to keep some tortoises as pets. The habitats and breeding beaches of tortoises and turtles are also being protected by turning them into nature reserves.

Tortoise and turtle fact

Turtle farms have been set up in China and Malaysia, and these help prevent wild turtles from being caught.

29

Life cycle of a turtle

Egg hatching

Juvenile

A female turtle is ready to breed when she is between 5 and 25 years old, depending on the species. She lays a clutch of eggs in the sand. A few months later, the hatchlings break out of the eggs. The young turtles gradually get larger. Most turtles live for 30 to 60 years, but some species live even longer.

Full-grown turtle

Glossary

ancient very, very old

camouflage coloring that blends in with the background

clutch bunch of eggs laid at the same time by a female animal

ectothermic having a body temperature that is similar to that of the surrounding environment

extinct not existing anymore, disappeared completely

habitat the place in which an animal or plant lives

hatchling name given to a young turtle or tortoise that has just emerged from the egg

hibernate go into a type of deep sleep during the cold winter months

migration a long journey made regularly by animals of the same species

predator an animal that hunts other animals

prey an animal that is hunted by another animal

reptile an animal that has a dry skin covered in scales. Most reptiles lay eggs

scale a hard flake that is attached to the skin of a reptile or fish

solitary living alone

species a group of animals that look alike and can breed together to produce young

terrapin a Native American word that should be used only for the diamond-backed terrapin, but is often used to desribe small freshwater turtles

tropical the parts of the world near the Equator that are hot all year round

vibration a small back-and-forth movement

Index